"I had always thought I had a thorough understanding of the role bees play in nature. But reading Dr. Reese Halter's book was a shocking revelation of the importance of bees in pollinating a wide variety of crops and plants, and thus their importance to our very survival. With amazing clarity and ease of understanding, Dr. Reese brings to light the vital role of bees in the pageant of all life on this planet. This is a "must read" for anyone concerned about the relationship of our ecology with our well-being. Thank you, Dr. Reese, for articulating the scientific knowledge in such an easily readable form."

— Courtney Milne, Master Photographer, author of *The Sacred Earth*

"In this book, Dr. Halter introduces us to the amazing honeybee. Not only do bees have sophisticated social organization and advanced communication and navigation skills, but they vote, dance and have strange sex. The book is written in a conversational style, with a myriad of interesting and often surprising facts (e.g., bees might be able to locate land mines and cure some cancers). The bee provides goodies for humans (e.g., honey, wax, medicines) but their main importance is as pollinators of food plants. Dr. Halter explains how bee populations recently have plummeted due to deforestation, contamination by insecticides, and disease. Our food supply is in peril. Dr. Halter presents a very convincing argument that we need to be doing a better job of looking after planet Earth. This is a good read, both informative and exciting. I thoroughly recommend it."

— Roger Sands, Professor Emeritus, University of Canterbury

"A fascinating narrative that exposes the profound importance of the humble honeybee to the well-being of all humans. Yet again Dr. Halter has exercised his ecological vision to interpret a crucial warning from the troubled world of bees. Get on board and be informed by this inspirational read as Dr. Reese takes us on a grand ride through the history of the natural world, exposes the pivotal role of bees in human endeavour and, although presaging decline, offers solutions and hope."

— Dr. Christopher J. Weston, Forest Ecology,
University of Melbourne

"Dr. Reese Halter is one of the most fascinating science writers of our time. In this book he has given us insight into the truly remarkable lives of bees. He will open your eyes to the incredible ways bees enhance our lives, how our relationships with them have lasted for thousands of years and how we have prospered as a result. Unfortunately, bees are now imperilled around the world, suffering from a mysterious deadly disease, their very survival in question. Dr. Reese explains the causes – and consequences – of their plight in an easily understandable way. I think *The Incomparable Honeybee* is essential reading for anyone interested in the wonders of the natural world."

— Robert O. Teskey, Distinguished Research Professor,
University of Georgia

"More than anyone I know, Dr. Reese Halter manifests the wise words of Senegalese poet Baba Dioum: to save nature, we must love it; to love it, we must understand it; to understand it, we must be taught. From understanding comes wonder, which Dr. Reese is a master at evoking."

— David Perry, Professor Emeritus, Oregon State University, co-author of *Forest Ecosystems*

"*The Incomparable Honeybee*, by Dr. Reese Halter, is a wonderfully fascinating book about the almost unimaginable services honeybees (and bees in general) perform for life on Earth. Every living species fulfills a vital service for the collective good of life, whether that service is visible or not, whether we understand it or not. *The Incomparable Honeybee* is a clarion wake-up call to the fact that each time a species is lost to extinction, we are compounding the impoverishment of every generation, beginning with our own children and grandchildren."

— Chris Maser, Zoologist, author of *Earth in our Care*

"If bees had hands they would applaud Dr. Halter for his highly readable yet authoritative treatment of their lives. This vastly important but little-understood group of insects has fuelled many parts of agriculture for millennia – but fuelled it quietly, fragrantly and tastefully. Quite the contrast from our own way of being. So this book will give people pause to reflect and rejoice in the miracle of bee-dom. Let the humm continue..."

— Professor Douglas W. Larson, University of Guelph, co-author of *The Last Stand*

The Incomparable Honeybee

&

The Economics
of Pollination

Dr. Reese Halter

RMB
Victoria Vancouver Calgary

Rocky Mountain Books
#108 – 17665 66A Avenue
Surrey, BC V3S 2A7
www.rmbooks.com

Rocky Mountain Books
PO Box 468
Custer, WA
98240-0468

Library and Archives Canada Cataloguing in Publication

Halter, Reese
    The incomparable honeybee and the economics of pollination / Reese Halter.

Includes bibliographical references.

ISBN 978-1-897522-60-8

    1. Honeybee. 2. Pollination by insects. 3. Honey. 4. Human-animal relationships. 5. Colony collapse disorder of honeybees. 6. Habitat conservation. I. Title.

QL568.A6H34 2009   595.79'9   C2009-903887-0

Printed and bound in Canada

Rocky Mountain Books gratefully acknowledges the financial support of the Government of Canada through the Book Publishing Industry Development Program (BPIDP); the Canada Council for the Arts; and the province of British Columbia through the British Columbia Arts Council and the Book Publishing Tax Credit for our publishing activities.

BRITISH COLUMBIA ARTS COUNCIL
Supported by the Province of British Columbia

Canada Council for the Arts   Conseil des Arts du Canada

The interior pages of this book have been produced on 100% post-consumer recycled paper, processed chlorine free and printed with vegetable-based dyes.

Mixed Sources
Cert no. SW-COC-001271
© 1996 FSC
FSC

For my mentor and hero:
my Dad, Aubrey J. Halter (1918–2008)

Contents

A Story of Reciprocation

This is a story about the most important pollinators on Earth – the remarkable bees. I cannot tell the bees' story in isolation, though, as it interweaves with those of humans and many ecological systems on our planet. The interreliant relationships these little creatures maintain are cause for great celebration and, currently, great concern. Over the past *three* years, a staggering number of bees have died – over 50 billion. This sad fact lends itself to an imperative discussion, one in which we increase our understanding of the reciprocation that is necessary to improve the health of bees, humans and our planet as a whole. With this enhanced knowledge, we must then take action to protect the remaining species of bees from extinction.

The story of the first bees began at least 100 million years ago – thus, it's a story 14 times older than that of the first human progenitors. Currently, there are approximately 20,000 named species of bees and perhaps as many as 40,000 kinds of bees worldwide. In North America alone – from the bitter cold of the Arctic Circle to the furnace-like Sonoran Desert – there are over 5,000 native species. No matter where in the world, regional plant life and bees have exquisitely adapted to flourish *together* in their specific environments.

To reproduce, flowers need bees to carry pollen from one to another – cross-pollination. Bees need the protein-rich pollen and vitamin-rich nectar from flowers for their reproductive processes, which vary in complexity between species. For instance, the most straightforward practice is that of the solitary bee species – the majority of bees worldwide. Solitary bees lay one egg in a nest packed with digested pollen and honey – a mix of dehydrated nectar with special bee ingredients – seal the hole and move on.

Honey, bumble and stingless bees, on the other hand, are social insects. Each bee has a specific role in a complex process of reproduction. Orchestration and co-operation are required, among a couple of hundred bees in the annual bumble bees to more than several thousand in stingless bees. Honeybees – our primary focus here – collaborate in colonies as large as 100,000 insects, in which one queen and many female workers govern. Intricate communication enables each colony to continuously respond to changing environmental factors. For example, the honeybees perform elaborate dances to detail and pinpoint newly discovered sources of food.

From honey hunters to the current wave of urban beekeepers, humans have also long appreciated the taste and health benefits of honey. For over 5,000 years, humans have kept honeybees in artificial hives. However, efficient storage was not available until 1851, when Reverend Lorenzo Langstroth, in Massachusetts, improved upon various European hive techniques and invented the perfect beekeeper hive. Consisting of two or three storeys with removable rectangular wooden frames, the Langstroth hive enables bees to build honeycomb and store honey in a suitable artificial environment.

Producing honey is not the only way honeybees contribute to human society, though. From the multi-use marvel of beeswax to potentially detecting and treating disease, the gifts humans receive from honeybees are phenomenal.

Often unknowingly, we are dependent on bees to do much more than produce goods of the hive. Bees pollinate over 100 crops in North America (and elsewhere). Economically, the total value of all bees' work is approximately $3-billion in Canada, $44-billion in the US and $2.3-billion in Australia. This fact is even more thought provoking if you consider what would happen if there were few of these species left. From fruits and vegetables to crops that support the beef and dairy industries, we rely on bees to pollinate over one-third of everything on our plates at mealtime. Beyond that, the cotton fields that lend part of their harvests to textile production also require these savvy pollinators. Unfortunately, agriculture as currently practised works against the natural environment and against the bees.

Despite this endless generosity of bees, humans have neglected their own role in this fragile relationship. Honeybees and humans share many similarities: we socialize, dance, eat honey, touch, feel, mimic one another, vote and get sick. But in recent years, bees' autoimmune systems have been shutting down and bee colonies have been collapsing. There is no single reason for this. Scientists believe it is instead a combination of biological and environmental factors, mass over-use of synthetic toxins and our antiquated agricultural system that are the culprits.

Bees are capable of helping humans when we fall ill and they provide for us at all times. In turn, we need to renew our commitment to this relationship. A tremendous amount is at stake. Until we properly reciprocate, we move closer toward eventual eradication of the bees, thus jeopardizing our own health and life as we know it on this planet.

As an intelligent, problem-solving species, we humans have choices to make. It is simply unacceptable that we allow the destruction of an estimated one species every 20 minutes of every day of every year. We must harness the hope that exists and help to subsidize the waves of change. To do this, we need to inform ourselves on the current situation and risks, understand what actions we can take as individuals and take action in every way possible. Understanding our interweaving stories is a first step in this right direction.

In the Beeginning

The history of bees begins with the evolution of plant life. While life on our planet began over 3.5 billion years ago, land plants have been around for about 400 million years. Giant horsetails, ferns, cycads and conifers – trees that bear cones and release naked seeds, such as pines and redwoods – all relied upon the wind to disseminate male pollen and assist in cross-pollinating plants. The prehistoric forests were so prolific that the billions of tons of organic matter accumulated in the Carboniferous Period – 354 to 290 million years ago – currently provides fossil fuels to most of humankind.

At the beginning of the Cretaceous Period – about 140 million years ago – land plants underwent a fantastic change. They grew colourful, pungent flowers filled with large, protein-rich pollen grains surrounded by nectar. Instead of relying on the wind to cross-pollinate these new flowering plants (angiosperms), nature conscripted insects – initially beetles and flies – by enticing them with the sweet and nutritious nectar. While feeding, these insects inadvertently brush against the male anther and transfer its pollen to an adjacent flower's receptive female stigma. The pollen fertilizes the ovule, which develops into a seed. Eventually, a fruit grows to enclose the seed(s).

By the end of the Cretaceous – about 65 million years ago – the diversity of plant life had exploded, adding over 21,000 angiosperms to about 3,000 species of conifers. Today, there are over 235,000 different species of angiosperms catalogued, whereas there are only 650 kinds of conifers remaining. Geologic upheavals and climate change have certainly had a hand in this change, but one particular insect has irrefutably assisted the angiosperms in conquering the land: bees. While flies, gnats, beetles, butterflies, moths, hummingbirds and bats are pollinators, too, bees conduct the lion's share of pollinating on Earth today.

The first bees evolved from predatory wasps about 100 million years ago. Bees specialized in feeding on the sweet carbohydrate nectar as a high energy source, which they eventually convert into honey. They also collect pollen as their only source of protein – a requisite for the development of offspring. When the bee lands on a flower, hairs of the positively charged bee attract the negatively charged pollen. This electrostatic charge is what enables most bees to be efficient pollinators. However, some workers deliberately make small packets of pollen using their saliva and store them inside the sidesaddle pouches on their hind legs – pollen baskets. Later, moving around inside another flower, bees unintentionally touch the female's stigma and pollinate it. None the wiser, they move on and continue their own quest for resources.

This interdependent relationship between flowering plants and their golden-haired pollination partners has grown ever more exclusive over time. For instance, the architecture of many flowers has adapted to allow only a bee's tongue to access the nectar. Most species of bees have subsequently witnessed a lengthening of their tongues over time.

The visible world is very different for bees, as they cannot see red but can detect ultraviolet (UV) light. Their unique visible spectrum grants bees access to a vibrant world in which some flowers that appear as one colour to humans actually have a much more intricate and colourful design. Almond flowers, for instance, use a neon colour visible only to bees, which guides the bees to receptive flowers.

Plants have also developed ingenious signals to inform pollinators when pollination has occurred. Many plant species use pungent floral scents to attract pollinators. Once pollinated, their scent dissipates. Some, like the vanilla orchid flower, fold up and appear desiccated within a half hour of pollination. Other flowers change colour once pollinated.

Native Bees of North America

The intimate relationship between bees and plants has thus far – mostly – served to ensure the survival of both. No matter what the geographical region, each species of plant and bee has adapted to the specific climate and characteristics of the area. Before we begin our specific discussion of honeybees, I want to take a moment to recognize other remarkable species of bees that brave the environment of North America, specifically the Great Plains Grassland.

The Great Plains Grassland occupies an astoundingly vast area of central North America, encompassing 14 per cent of the total area of Canada and the US. The story of this prairie land is one that revolves around climate. A land of extremes, the prairies are either inundated by glacial meltwater or dry as a bone. A vast and hardy assemblage of more than 2,000 species of plants and animals are native to the prairies. Almost 70 per cent of these plants depend upon various species of solitary and bumble bees to assist them with cross-pollination.

In fact, nearly 25 per cent of the native plants on the Great Plains Grassland have evolved *with* specific species of native bumble bees. In Missouri, for example, the long-tongued black and yellow bumble bee (*Bombus nevadensis*) services – almost exclusively – the wild berga-mot plant. The eastern bumble bee (*Bombus impatiens*) cross-pollinates only the spikes of Culver's root with its specially adapted short tongue. Solitary bees too have formed almost ex-clusive relationships with some crop plants. For instance, the squash and gourd bees mate, sleep and dine on their respectively named plants. I have seen pumpkin bees chewing their way out of a wilted flower in the morning in order to get to the next open flower. Two species of solitary bees, the alkali bee (*Nomia melanderi*) and the alfalfa bee (*Megachile pacifica*), are conscripted in commercial alfalfa seed production, which then feeds millions of cattle.

Distinctions between honey, bumble and solitary bees often seem blurred to the untrained eye, but the unique characteristics of each are vital for pollinating different types of plants. For instance, whereas honeybees drink nectar from the side of some plants, solitary and bumble bees will snap open the floral heads and exchange pollen while they sip on the nectar. However, bumble bees also are known "nectar robbers" because they sometimes tear a hole in the corolla (all the petals) of a flower to extract the nectar. Whenever this larcenous activity occurs, the bee fails to trip the flower's pollination mechanism. Thus, no seeds are set and the flower must wait for a more obedient bee – perhaps of a different species – to happen along.

Several factors are currently threatening the native bees of North America. While I will address these issues farther on, for now I want to plant a few seeds of thought. As you continue reading, perhaps begin to think about how each of these issues is harmful to bee populations. For starters, climate change is affecting the timing, or phenology, of plant flowering, which is often occurring earlier in the season. Destruction of natural habitat has been rampant in recent decades, as has widespread application of synthetic herbicides and pesticides. All these things are having a deleterious effect on our native bees.

Not only do these factors harm bee populations, but many species are actually being wiped out altogether. Limiting the consideration only to species of bumble bees, the list – so far – is grim. Since 1999, the rusty-patched bumble (*Bombus affinis*) – whose habitat spanned from Quebec to Vermont – has disappeared, along with four other bumble bee species. Franklin's bumble bee (*Bombus franklini*) of northern California and southern Oregon is also now believed to be extinct. And the once large population of the western bumble bee (*Bombus occidentalis*) that inhabited the entire west coast of North America – from Alaska to California – has severely declined in the past decade.

Bumble Bees

We all know the title of this manifesto is *The Incomparable Honeybee*, so why is this section about bumble bees? Well, my reasoning is two-fold. First, all species of bees are important in a multitude of ways. That said, having knowledge of another type of bee enhances the ability to appreciate the matchlessly complex society and behaviour of the honeybees. Through comparison, we see how the honeybees are truly incomparable. So, let's take a quick look at the life cycle and attributes of the bumble bee.

There are about 60 species of bumble bees in which each individual weighs an average of half a gram, or at least two-and-a-half times more than a queen honeybee. Although a colony of bumble bees may visit a wide variety of flowers during the course of a season, an individual bee visits only one species of plant on a single trip away from the nest. Bumble bees visit two to three times more flowers than honeybees during a 15-hour workday. Despite living in colonies – like honeybees – bumble bees do not have an intricate system of communication. Rather, they work in solitude – tirelessly starting before dawn and often finishing after sunset in cool and sometimes inhospitable environs.

While most bees are proficient pollinators, bumble and some solitary bees perform an even more astounding fertilization feat called buzz pollination, or sonification. Buzz pollination entails a bee grabbing hold of a flower and curling up her abdomen – the rearward segments of a bee that contain its digestive and reproductive organs – to form a c shape. Closing her wings over her thorax, or mid-section, the bee shivers her strong flight muscles to create a sonic vibration. This robust vibration shakes the flower and, importantly, the male anthers, where the pollen is stored. A copious amount of pollen dislodges from the anthers and coats the bee by means of the electrostatic attraction. The bee then grooms and moves on to continue foraging; invariably, pollen reaches the female stigma of another flower. Pollination accomplished!

These bees' magnificent sonification technique is responsible for the pollination of – to name only a few – sunflowers, canola, rapeseed, lentils, peas, tomatoes, chilies, red clover and alfalfa. Commercial greenhouses have tried tools such as electric vibration wands to replicate buzz pollination by bees, but such manual pollination techniques increase costs and produce significantly lower yields. In Australia the lack of native bumble bees on the mainland posed a challenge for interested parties such as greenhouse growers. Efforts to import bumble bees were resisted due to past issues with non-native species in the country, so researchers began focusing instead on native species – blue-banded bees – that are capable of similar sonification. With more than 8 per cent of the 235,000 flowering plant species in the world relying on the unique buzz pollination technique to reproduce, the importance of bumble and solitary bees is clear.

These prodigious workers are able to fly in snowstorms, wind and rain at 11–20 kilometres per hour (7 to 12 miles per hour). Even when a bumble bee has two full pollen baskets, which add about 20 per cent more weight, or 100 milligrams, to its body – it can fly as far as 6 kilometres (3.7 miles) from the nest. The bumble bee uses the same aerodynamic principle as helicopters with reverse-pitch semi-rotary blades do: each time a bumble bee's wings swing back and forth (one oscillation cycle), a type of cavity or vacuum is produced in the air above the wing. This cavity provides extra lift for the large bumble bee and her load of pollen.

A bumble bee, however, cannot lift off unless her body is warmer than 35°C (95°F). If she lives at the frigid Arctic Circle – for instance – the only possible food source that could give her enough energy is honey. In fact, it takes a honey-fuelled bumble bee only seconds to rev up her body temperature from 20°C (68°F) to 35°C – an extraordinary achievement accomplished by shivering her musculature. On the other hand, if a bumble bee's body temperature exceeds 44°C (111°F) it uses its abdomen to transfer heat and cool off.

The defence behaviour of bumble bees is not seen in either stingless or honeybees. Despite seeming rather docile, a bumble bee will raise her middle legs when she is bothered while mildly at rest or perched. If further annoyed, the bumble bee will roll on her back, brace her body and point her stinger while opening her mouth. Since bumble bees do not have barbed stingers, they are able to sting repeatedly. Predators – like skunks, shrikes and foxes – receive extra treatment, as bumble bees spray feces and vomit honey on them.

Typically, a colony of bumble bees is annual. Each spring, the queen bumble bee emerges from her eight-month hibernation. Upon waking, her first order of business is to find flowers to provide her with nectar and pollen. Inseminated the previous fall, she also collects pollen to fertilize her first eggs. Using grasses or the inside of an old mouse den, she builds a nest. From her wax gland, the queen makes a small honey pot and regurgitates the nectar into it. After laying eight to ten eggs in the nest, the queen covers it with a waxen canopy that, despite the chilly spring air, maintains a temperature of 30°C (86°F). The queen then sits on the brood – much like a hen – and sips from the honey pot all night long.

In the morning, she breaks the waxen nest cover and shivers to warm her body up to 35°C (95°F). She then darts off to collect more honey and pollen. After three days, the eggs hatch. The queen feeds these new female workers honey and pollen for the next 16 to 25 days, after which they are mature. During their meagre two weeks of life after matura-tion, these bees are responsible for collecting nectar and pollen, making wax pots and help-ing with second-generation eggs. The queen's last batch of eggs produces approximately 100 queens and 100 drones. At the end of the season, the queen dies. The process begins again with a new queen that emerges in the last batch of eggs.

The life expectancy of a colony of bumble bees – usually with a population of no more than 400 individuals – depends on the length of the growing season. For instance, queen bumble bees that live at the Arctic Circle – where the growing season is relatively short – emerge at 0°C (32°F) and live for no longer than two-and-a-half months. Conversely, in Central and South America, some bumble bee species can live for up to two years and colonies can reach a population of 2,000 individuals.

The Complex Society of Honeybees

While the majority of bees worldwide are solitary or have colonies of independent workers, honeybees co-operate in a complex society within their colony or hive. The hive can contain as many as 100,000 individuals, but one queen bee rules the colony by constantly emitting at least 18 pheromones, or hormones.

Under the queen's rule, a highly efficient organization exists in which all members work for the common good. The workers in the hive are all females, with only about 200 to 300 males, or drones, at any one time during the summer months. The queen, workers and drones have different roles to play. While the queen and the drones maintain one function from birth, worker bees progress through a series of different responsibilities.

The body of a honeybee consists of a series of hardened plates covered with dense hairs. Most of its vital organs – including the venomous barbed stinger – are inside the bee's abdomen. It has a head with three smaller eyes that detect polarized light, enabling bees to use the sun as a compass. Two larger, hairy, compound eyes help determine wind flow and colours – including UV radiation, violet blue, blue green, green yellow and orange, but not red. A worker bee's head has two antennae loaded with 3,000 sensory organs. Their ability to distinguish more than 170 odours is vital for smelling nectar, pollen, water, tree resin and alert pheromones.

The honeybee's midsection, or thorax, has three pairs of legs and two sets of wings. The six hairy legs are important for walking, prying flowers open, dancing on the comb and grooming. The hind legs contain pollen baskets, or corbicula. The two pairs of wings beat at 200 cycles per second and defy the rules of aerodynamics in their masterful ability to allow a honeybee to travel at speeds greater than 24 kilometres per hour (15 miles per hour) for up to

13 kilometres (8 miles) at a time. During flight, the honeybee is able to maintain a thorax temperature of an astonishing 46°C (115°F) by passing the excess heat to its head by regurgitating droplets of watered-down honey, cooling the head off just as sweat does in mammals.

The queen makes pipping sounds and lays about 1,500 eggs per day, or between 175,000 and 200,000 per year. Normally, she is able to perform her role for about four years. Six to ten young bees, usually less than 12 days old, surround her. They constantly examine the queen with their antennae and forelegs, while licking her with their hairy tongues. After the queen lays about 30 eggs, they feed and groom her and remove her feces. The queen's retinue manufactures a protein- and lipid-rich royal jelly from two different sets of glands in their heads, which they pass to the queen in a direct mouth-to-mouth action. Royal jelly contains vitellogenin, an indispensable protein that boosts the immune defence system, reduces stress and acts as a potent antioxidant to help reduce wear and tear throughout the queen's body.

After three days, the eggs hatch. Young bees, known as nurse bees, feed the larvae royal jelly – analogous to mother's milk – for three days. After that, the nurse bees feed the larvae a mixture of pollen and honey called bees' bread. Bees' bread contains lactic acid bacteria that ferment the pollen to make it more nutritious, digestible and mould-resistant than raw pollen. By the seventh day of feeding, the larvae have increased their weight 500-fold since birth. If this occurred in humans, the average newborn baby would weigh 1,360 kilograms (or a ton and a half!).

On the ninth day of their life cycle, the larvae finish eating and spin a cocoon. The nurse bees make a wax in their abdomen to cap the hexagonal cocoon cell and enable the larvae to complete their development. Twenty-one days later, the larvae have become worker bees and they chew through the waxen cell cap, emerge and immediately begin to clean their cell. With the assistance of 15 to 30 workers, one cell takes a bee, on average, 41 minutes to prepare. The vitality of the colony relies on this process, as the queen will only lay eggs in cells that are clean.

Drones – born in late summer – emerge after 24 days. Nurse bees must feed them for about a week, but after that they must provide for themselves. These male bees are larger than workers but smaller than queens, and do not possess stingers. Drones have only one role in the colony, which most never fulfill: to inseminate virgin queens. Their eyes are very large and their antennae are ten times more sensitive than worker bees', each equipped with 30,000 sensory receptors especially adapted for smelling virginal queens. For the duration of their three-week lives, they exit the hive at midday and congregate with drones from different colonies before returning in late afternoon.

From a very young age, the worker honeybee has a phenomenal ability to multi-task. Throughout her life – of less than 60 days – she may perform as many as 20 tasks. For instance, a young bee will tend to the nursery, clean brood cells, patrol the hive on sanitation duty and assist at capping the comb. Capping one comb takes six hours and hundreds of workers. Before a young bee graduates to one of the most remarkable (and not yet fully understood) feats of nature – the perfect construction of a honeycomb – she will greet an older forager bee. The forager stores nectar collected from flowers in a special compartment in her abdomen called the honey crop. She returns to the hive and passes the nectar along to – usually – three young receiving bees.

The nectar is comprised mostly of water and as much as 20 per cent sugar. The receiver bee moves to a less crowded area of the hive and repeatedly folds and unfolds her mouthparts, exposing the nectar to air to evaporate the water. At the same time, she secretes the enzyme invertase to help transform the nectar into honey. She then places the dehydrated nectar into a cell to further reduce the water content below 18 per cent. Other worker bees fan the open cells at 24,500 wing-beats per minute. After a couple of days, the nectar is now honey and ready to be sealed or capped in the cell.

Honey, with its high caloric energy, is the fuel of the hive. One kilogram (2.2 pounds) contains about 3,250 calories. Compared to the same weight of apples (400 calories), oranges (230) or cucumbers (140), honey is essentially rocket fuel. One teaspoon of honey weighing 21 grams contains 16 grams of sugar, or 60 calories. It takes 12 honeybees a combined flying distance of over 9,600 kilometres (5,965 miles) – and their entire foraging lives – to produce that 21 grams of honey. Worldwide, the species of honeybee that is the Clydesdale workhorse of honeymaking is the Italian honeybee (*Apis mellifera*).

Colonies store much more nectar than pollen. Pollen contains between 6 and 20 per cent protein and is vital for the growing young of the colony. It takes 15 to 50 kilograms (33 to 110 pounds) of pollen a year – compared to 60 to 80 kilograms (132 and 176 pounds) of honey – to maintain a hive for one year. This translates into one million trips for pollen and four million trips for nectar by foraging bees. Some forager workers unload pollen baskets to young receiver workers, who in turn treat the pollen with a phytocidal acid to prevent germination. This treatment enables the pollen to be mixed with honey as bees' bread capped in cells.

It takes 66,000 bee-hours of activity to produce the 77,000 splendid hexagonal cells that form the comb of the hive. Almost 9 kilograms (20 pounds) of honey are required for a young worker bee to produce one kilogram (2.2 pounds) of beeswax. Bees eat the honey and trigger a gland in their abdomen to secrete wax. The bees then chew the wax flakes to soften them. One kilogram of this hearty wax can support 22 kilograms (48 pounds) of honey, or more than 20 times its own weight. Many decades ago, the aeronautics industry recognized the strength of honeycomb and adapted nature's design to enhance the bending and stiffness of aircraft wings, as the wings must support heavy loads of fuel in the aircraft.

To construct the honeycomb, hair plates at the base of a bee's neck act as a plumb bob to determine the changing orientation to gravity. When a worker bee turns relative to the earth's gravitational field, the pressure of the hair plates on its legs tells the bee which way is up. Without these hair plates, workers could not build honeycomb. When honeybees were transported into outer space on the 1984 Challenger shuttle flight, they were unable to construct honeycomb, due to the lack of gravitational force.

Workers use the tip of their antennae to assess the thickness and smoothness of comb cells, but the exactness of the cell diameters and their orientation is still not explained. Bees construct honeycomb horizontally. Amazingly, chambers are back to back at exactly a 13-degree angle to prevent honey from dripping out.

Propolis is the glue that bees use to cement and enhance the strength of the comb base. They also extensively coat the entire hive nest cavity with a thin waterproofing and insulating antifungal and antibacterial layer. To make propolis, bees combine enzymes from their mouths with the pollen, nectar, water and tree resin. Propolis also patches holes, prevents ants from invading and embalms intruders that are too large for the bees to remove from the hive. If a mouse enters the hive, the bees sting it to death and use propolis to mummify it, therefore protecting the colony from bacteria that would otherwise flourish on the dead rodent.

Within the comb, storage and space allocation is meticulous. Storing honey near the points where the comb attaches minimizes the potential stress that such a heavy substance could cause to the wax comb at the top of the hive. The nursery is located in cells that allow maintenance of the temperature in the central part of the comb. Larger drone cells take space along the comb edges.

Honeybees are extremely hygienic. About one per cent of all workers are constantly on sanitation duty, removing mouldy pollen, old cell caps, dead workers or deadbeat drones.

After young comb-building workers graduate, their first job outside is to provide a fan or exhaust system for the hive. Hundreds of bees work just outside the hive entrance by fanning their wings at 24,500 beats a minute to help cool the colony and remove carbon dioxide. When the colony temperature exceeds 35°C (95°F), forager bees bring loads of water into the hive and pass them to receiver bees. The receiver bees tongue-lash the water onto developing eggs and honeycomb while nurse bees fan their wings to create an ingenious evaporative cooling system.

Fanning bees later graduate to become guard bees. As the name implies, they patrol outside the hive and closely scrutinize every forager bee upon its arrival back at the hive. Guard bees stand on their back four legs with antennae held forward and forelegs lifted. They ascertain the odour and behaviour of every bee entering. If they detect trouble, they emit an alarm pheromone that quickly signals a red alert. When honey hunters and beekeepers use smoke on a hive, it is to dilute this pheromone.

Worker bees have barbed stingers that detach from their abdomens but continue to inject venom into victims for up to one minute. A furious honeybee will sting in the same place repeatedly. The stinger is a honeybee's main source of defence. Once released, she dies.

About 25 per cent of the colony workers are forager bees, the oldest workers. They average 10 to 15 trips a day, but as many as 150 trips are possible. Visiting between one and one thousand flowers of the same species in a day, a one-way trip can be as far as 13 kilometres (8 miles). Forager bees work themselves to death, as after 800 kilometres (497 miles) their bodies simply stop functioning.

Thirty five per cent of the foragers are scout bees, constantly on the lookout for new sources of nectar, pollen, tree resin and water. Scouts are also responsible for identifying a new location for the hive when it is time to swarm. When the strength of the queen's pheromones diminishes, nurse bees feed about half a dozen larvae only royal jelly as they begin to rear a new queen. In the meantime, scout bees find a new location. They reach a consensus on a new location by voting. Research has shown that 15 is the crucial number of scout bees for a quorum. Then they wait for the signal to evacuate.

Taking about half of the colony with her, the reigning queen travels in the centre of the swarm. It takes about 40 days for the bees to build a new hive. Timing is very important, as in most cases there are not enough flowers in bloom for a late summer swarm to successfully build comb and have enough stored honey to last the winter.

Meanwhile, back at the old hive the first new queen to hatch has a pressing task to complete: to murder all competing soon-to-be-emerging queens. Once she has secured her position, she undertakes her only flight out of the nest. Releasing as little as a billionth of a gram of her scent, she attracts drones. The queen may mate with a couple dozen drones, storing as much as seven million sperm – enough to last her a lifetime. The drones take three seconds to ejaculate before their penis is ripped out of their body, after which – writhing in pain – they die.

The last batch of bees to hatch before winter must gorge themselves on protein and lipid-rich pollen-based bees' bread. The protein enables them to store vitellogenin in their bodies so they can provide royal jelly to the queen and her first eggs that hatch in the springtime.

About a quarter of the bees in a hive over winter are constantly shivering and moving in a concentric circle around the queen. Similar to the emperor penguins of the South Pole, they utilize the warmth of the thermal mass. Every bee takes turns in the warmest central part of the circular mass, as those on the outside repeatedly shuffle into the centre and then back out to the exterior. The temperature in the hive never drops below 18°C (64°F).

Intricate Steps of Communication

Communication among bees varies by species. For example, the meliponine stingless bees communicate with one another by transmitting sound signals. Duration and frequencies of these sounds translate into information about distances to new food, water and tree resin sources.

In order for a social society like honeybees to thrive, they must also constantly communicate new information about the colony and its current requirements. Honeybees communicate by dancing. Each performed dance taps into the amazing ability honeybees possess to rapidly switch foraging tasks based on the immediate needs of the hive. Up-to-date information dictates whether worker bees are to forage for nectar, pollen, water or tree resin.

Nobel laureate Karl von Frisch (1886–1982) dedicated his life to unravelling many of the mysteries of the honeybee. He was the first researcher to decipher the purposeful and endearing dancing of bees. Decades of subsequent research revealed four primary dances: the *round*, *c-shaped*, *waggle* and *vibrational* dances, and at least five other, less-understood dances. While sometimes performed outside on the surface of the swarm, dances are more likely to happen inside the hive, near the entrance on the vertical comb or farther inside in total darkness. In the latter case, the bees rely on their acute senses of smell, taste and touch to interpret the dance.

When a scout or forager bee finds a rich blossom patch, it sips every drop of nectar from deep within the flower, using her long, hairy, straw-like tongue, or glossa. Then she turns her scent pocket inside out, saturating it with the pungent floral aroma. The scent pocket is a damp, glistening pad tucked inside a small fold of skin near the tip of a bee's tail.

When the excited worker arrives back at the hive, she finds usually three receiver bees to off-load most of the nectar. She then performs a dance indicating the new source of nectar. If the blossoms are within 10 metres (33 feet) of the hive, the bee performs the *round* dance. First, she will exchange a few drops of nectar so the other bees can taste it. Then she starts spinning around in a narrow circle, changing direction to the right and then the left, dancing one or two circles in each direction.

Other bees follow the dancer very closely. Their antennae touch and smell her scent gland and thousands of her hairs containing nectar residue. Twenty or more dance recitals can take place, with the dances lasting between a few seconds and a minute. The longer the dance, the more workers she recruits.

If the nectar is between 10 and 100 metres (33 and 328 feet) from the hive, the scout will perform a *c-shaped* dance. This dance is quite similar to the round dance, except, of course, the scout never completes an entire circle. The c-shaped and round dances do not give workers an exact nectar location. Rather, they communicate that the bounty is within close proximity of the hive. Bees' powerful sense of smell may then guide them to the new floral source.

The *waggle* dance is one of the most extraordinary forms of communication in the entire animal kingdom. This dance conveys precise information about the food's location, including its direction and the distance from the hive – as far as 13 kilometres (8 miles). In his research, von Frisch determined that workers assess critical fragments of information from each of the dance's components, including the duration of waggling and buzzing; the length of the straight run, in comb cell diameters; the number of unit circuits per dance; and the average distance of the dances from the hive entrance.

The waggle dance follows a nearly figure-eight shape, but with a straight (bee)line connecting the two semicircles. The scout runs along a narrow semicircle, making sharp turns, and then beelines straight back to her starting point. She then performs the same moves in the opposite direction. The dance is elaborate, with the bee waggling her abdomen in precise, intricate steps.

At each turn she vigorously shakes her body: the side to side waggle occurs about 13 to 15 times a second and gives off a buzzing sound as her muscles and skeleton vibrate.

At the end of a complete dance, the scout will stop and share nectar with other workers, who extend their antennae to smell the dancer. Some new followers even squeak, causing the dancer to stop mid-stream and feed them a droplet of nectar.

Dance tempo and beeline length indicate distance from the hive to the flowers. That is, followers assess the distance by measuring the number of circuits per 15 seconds and the amount of time spent waggling and buzzing on the straight run. A slow dance tempo and long straight run communicate that the distance is greater. It does not convey exact distance, but informs the other bees of the amount of energy needed to find the new resource. This translates into the amount of honey each forager must eat before leaving the hive. The waggle dance can also inform foragers about new sources of water, tree resin and pollen.

The extent of the waggling, the total number of dance cycles and the intensity of the buzzing vibrations all work together to communicate the quality of the flowers at the new source. The richer the nectar, the greater the intensity of these three attributes. The longer an entire waggle dance sequence is, the larger the size of the floral patch.

Fascinatingly, the waggle dance – mostly performed in the dark and on the vertical face of the comb – somehow conveys the horizontal direction to the food source. Research suggests that if the dancer's beelines move straight up the hive wall, foragers should fly toward the sun to find the source. Running straight down the wall means they must fly away from the sun. Amazingly, the dancer will match the movement of the sun during the dance by modifying the angle of the beeline.

Specialized organs at the base of a bee's neck are able to detect the gravitational angle of the dance and translate this information into the angle of the sun to the horizon. When bees exit the colony, they use the sun as their compass.

If it is cloudy or the sun has moved, they use a time correction factor to account for the sun's movement. In addition, honeybees are able to detect polarized light that penetrates clouds, acting as a backup navigational system to help track the sun. On a night of a full moon, workers continue to dance after dark – somehow compensating for the movement of the sun after sundown.

The fact that bees possess a memory for time is intriguing. Interestingly, von Frisch was able to train bees to arrive at feeding stations on three, four and five separate periods within 24 hours.

If there are crosswinds upon exiting the hive, honeybees turn their bodies indirectly into the wind to minimize resistance and economize on honey consumption. To return to the hive, they may use a number of landmarks such as trees, rock formations or barns to help guide them.

The fourth dance is the *vibrational* dance, where a worker vibrates her abdomen while holding the queen or a co-worker. This dance indicates either foraging or swarming activities. Pollen foragers use the vibrational dance to speed up other workers or convey information about daily and seasonal food availability, such as peaks. The vibrational dance can also alert the queen that nurse bees have begun to raise new queens. A few hours before swarming, the vibrational dance ceases throughout the entire colony. Once the swarm has departed, the remaining workers begin the vibrational dance once again – increasing the intensity after the first new queen has emerged.

The other dances von Frisch elaborated on include *jostling*, *spasmodic*, *buzzing run*, *shaking* and *trembling*. During the jostling dance, successful foragers return to the hive and jostle their co-workers by running and pushing them toward the "dance floor." The spasmodic dance functions to distribute food, but interspersed brief waggles signal a pending new-resource dance. The buzzing run denotes swarming. A shaking dance, which takes place from side to side, is a request from a co-worker for assistance in grooming. Finally, the exact function of the series of twitches, trembles and running on four legs called the trembling dance is unknown.

Researchers continue to explore the meanings and functions of these extraordinary dances of honeybees. Investigating how cocaine use exaggerates the dances of a forager bee has led a University of Illinois research team to suggest that there is a reward system in bees' brains. Other research focuses on the differences in dances between comparative samples of honeybee populations with more or less stress, such as habitat destruction or pesticide exposure. While the magnificent dances of honeybees communicate information to each other, humans can watch, listen and learn from their messages as well.

The Gifts They Give Us

The energy that honeybees invest into communication, foraging, production and reproduction also provides humans with many benefits. There are several notable examples throughout history that illustrate the timeless generosity of bees. From energy-rich, medicinally beneficial honey to beeswax, humans continually reap the benefits of honeybees' hard work. Yet, as we will see, the giving does not end there.

Honey

Open a "pot of gold(en)" honey and some of the first osmophores, or scent molecules, reflect petals of the nectar-providing flowers. The colour, scent and taste of honey differ depending on the local environment. Some, like Californian heather or Oregon buckwheat, are dark, while others such as Quebec's dandelion honey are straw-coloured. From the Ohi'a tree's creamy Hawaiian Lehua to the water-like British Columbian or Alaskan fireweed, each honey has its own character. Australia's wonderfully spicy leatherwood honey stands in total contrast with the herbal tasting eucalyptus. My favourite honey – and the title of a melodious 1971 song by Van Morrison – is tupelo honey. Its heavenly burnt-sugar tang comes from the tupelo trees in the swamps of Georgia and Florida.

Over 1.2 billion kilograms (2.65 billion pounds) of honey are produced each year. Honey contains over 200 substances. Bees secrete a glucose oxidase enzyme that assists in converting nectar into honey. Along with oxygen, the glucose enzyme splits the glucose molecule into water and hydrogen peroxide. Due to its hydrogen peroxide and glucose oxidase content, honey is a powerful antiseptic. High amounts of malic, citric, tartaric, oxalic and other organic acids combined with the enzymes catalase and peroxidase give honey its renowned antibacterial properties.

The ancient Mayans revered the stingless honeybees, and a thousand-year-old document of theirs, the Madrid Codex, pictures shamans successfully treating cataracts, conjunctivitis, chills and fever with honey-based medicines. With over 80 per cent sugar content and its natural acidity, honey creates an inhospitable environment for the single-celled microbes that form infections. The low water content of honey keeps bacteria, which thrive in water, from flourishing. Ancient Greeks and Romans had also discovered these properties of honey; they used honey to treat cataracts and heal open wounds. Some modern bandage companies line their products with diluted traces of honey.

Honey – in conjunction with wax – is also effective as an embalming fluid. Ancient Egyptians, Persians, Babylonians, Assyrians and Arabs preserved their important dead in this way. Even the ancient Greek king Alexander the Great – who died on foreign soil – is said to have arrived back home in Macedonia immersed in a honey-filled coffin.

The preservative power of honey also works to its own advantage, as demonstrated by the sealed jars recovered from Egyptians' royal tombs that were found unspoiled, after thousands of years.

Honey is loaded with vitamins and minerals. It contains water-soluble B1, B2, B6, pantothenic and nicotinic acids, vitamin C – as well as high amounts of fat-soluble vitamins E, K and A. Honey also provides us with essential minerals: calcium, phosphorus, potassium, iron, copper, manganese, magnesium and sulfur. Some of these minerals in the specific concentrations found in honey mimic the concentration of blood serum. Thus, honey metabolizes easily and can be an important source of essential nutrients. In addition, the combination of glucose and fructose (monosaccharides) and some maltose, melezitose and dextrin makes honey an excellent source of caloric energy.

Some researchers suggest that a teaspoon or two of honey before bed ensures a restorative sleep. A human liver stores about eight hours of glycogen – an important brain food. If you eat supper at 7 pm, by about 3 am your brain releases a stress hormone called cortisol. Cortisol scavenges the body, melts muscle tissue and converts it into glycogen to feed the brain. When released, cortisol causes the heart to beat faster and raises glucose insulin levels in the blood. Elevated cortisol can lead to obesity, diabetes, coronary disease and autoimmune breakdown. A teaspoon of honey at night fuels the liver with glucose and fructose, which is absorbed slowly – thus providing a restful sleep and preventing the release of cortisol. Honey's low glycemic index enables diabetics to also enjoy the reputed sleep benefits. Particularly, Floridian tupelo and New Zealand manuka honeys are best for diabetics. Children over the age of 2 can also benefit from honey, as it promotes learning and stimulates the area of developing tissue at the end of the long bones, called growth plates.

Importantly, we must be cautious when deciding which honey to purchase. In 2002, China, supplying the US with almost a third of its honey, shipped 70,000 kilograms

(154,000 pounds) of honey contaminated with chloroamphenicol. The compound is banned in Australia, Canada, Europe, New Zealand and the United States, because although it treats anthrax, it also causes bone marrow failure through aplastic anemia. The Sara Lee Corporation, unknowingly, bought that contaminated honey and marketed a half million loaves of bread containing it. The next year, China finally banned chloroamphenicol.

We cannot know how many other banned, toxic and carcinogenic chemicals are in use, so always ensure that the honey you purchase carries a recognized organic certified seal.

Honey Hunters Then and Still

Modern appreciation of honey follows on the heels of an intriguing history. Early humans may have first discovered honey by observing other animals pursue the sweet riches. Chimpanzees in Africa, for instance, insert a stick or their hand into the bees' hive and remove it dripping with honey. The apes also use tools to break away wood around the flight hole in order to extract parts of the honeycomb. A number of other animals, including bears, skunks, foxes and honey buzzards, relish the energy-rich honey from the hives of bees.

One of the most intriguing honey-seeking partnerships is that of the African honeyguide bird and the ratel, or honey badger. The honeyguide has an unmistakable chirp that guides the ratel to a hive. The badger has strong legs, a thick hide that is impenetrable by bee stings, and paws specifically designed to rip apart honeybee nests. Once the badger has eaten its share of the honey and comb, the honeyguide moves in and eats the beeswax. Co-attackers, such as ants and small mammals, then consume any leftover larvae and honey.

To defend their territory, honeybees use potent stingers. The stingless honeybees of Middle and South America, Australia and Indonesia defend their hives by attacking intruders' eyes, nose and ears. Some species even developed a mechanism for squirting a caustic fluid toward their attacker. Early honey hunters learned to carry smoldering vegetation to drive bees away and pacify them, allowing hunters to successfully loot honey caches. A successful raid could result in a bounty of wax, propolis (bee glue), bee larvae (which provides a small amount of animal protein) and up to 45 kilograms (99 pounds) of honey.

Honey hunting may date millions of years back into the Paleolithic period (Old Stone Age), but certainly took place during the Mesolithic period (Middle Stone Age). Depicted on cave walls around the world, the hunt for honey was – and still is – an important facet of many peoples and cultures.

Among other functions, caves offered these nomadic hunters and gatherers a space to communicate and keep records through drawings carved into the rock walls, called petroglyphs. Archeologists have documented almost 400 sites in 17 regions, including Europe, North and South Africa, India, Malaysia, Indonesia and Australia, where ancient peoples recorded the cherished honey hunt in detailed petroglyphs.

There is an incredible mysticism about this art. Some of the pictorial histories illustrate an aggressive hunt, while others show the bees almost *allowing* the extraction of their wares by these intrepid honey hunters. Rituals associated with the honey hunt often seem mysterious and spiritual. Researchers hypothesize that some hunters were actually clan shamans, reputed to have supernatural powers.

The first paintings of Mesolithic honey hunters to be discovered – in the 1920s – were the petroglyphs in the Cave of Spiders in Valencia, Spain. In the primary illustration, two figures are perched precariously on a vine ladder. The figure at the top – a collection basket tied to his waist – is raiding a hive. Over-large bees surround the hunter. The figure halfway up the ladder looks to be in awe, gazing up at the hunter.

Drawn around the same time as the Cave of Spiders images, the petroglyphs at Barranc Fondo in eastern Spain are far richer in detail. The image shows 11 detailed figures, including animals, standing at the base of a tree awaiting five honey hunters who are on a large ladder. Mystical creatures are hovering near the hive while swarms of bees attack the honey hunters. Two hunters are falling off the ladder, perhaps in agony from bee stings.

In central India too there is mesmerizing and colourful cave art that vividly documents how central the ritual of honey hunting was. The intricate details may actually have been a form of visualization, thus ensuring a triumphant hunt. The giant honeybees of India (*Apis dorsata*) are gregarious nesters, with some trees supporting over 200 colonies.

On the African continent, there are more honey-hunting petroglyphs than anywhere else in the world. The Drakensberg Mountains of South Africa have over 40,000 paintings in 500 caves, spanning 3,000 years.

The direct descendants of those ancient honey hunters are the San peoples of present-day South Africa. Their spiritual nighttime ritual – as it was for their ancestors as well – is to dance for hours at the base of the hive tree, hypnotically humming into a deep trance. The hum of the San peoples is very similar to the vibrational thrum of the honeybees, perhaps enabling the San to calm the soon to be raided hives.

Another significant honey-hunting African people are the pygmies, currently numbering about 150,000. Their relatively small average height of 1.5 metres (4 feet 11 inches) allows manoeuvrability that works to their advantage during honey hunting. The Central African Aka pygmies hunt both honeybees and stingless honeybees for two months each year. Parties of five, including children, search the forest floor for ant nests near trees. Bees naturally die and fall to the foot of hive trees. Ants then carry off their bodies, dismember them in their nests and discard the inedible exoskeletons. Pygmy search parties look for these small middens glimmering in shafts of sunlight just outside the ants' entrance holes.

Once they identify a hive tree, the pygmies scan the trunk for an entrance hole. The honey hunter, an axe on his back and charcoal smeared on his face to protect himself from the forth-coming stings, uses lengths of vine to climb the tree. Tied to his waist is another length of vine which he uses to haul up smouldering wood wrapped in wet leaves.

As the hunter approaches the nest, he blows smoke into the hole to help calm the bees still in the hive. Many furious bees quickly exit to defend their territory by repeatedly stinging his mostly bare body. The hunter taps the bark to skilfully determine the exact location of the hive. Bracing himself against the trunk, with the vines for support, he chips away at the trunk with his axe.

Once the hole is large enough, the hunter reaches inside the hive and faces a second wave of infuriated bees. Somehow managing to disregard the painful stings, he carefully breaks off pieces of honeycomb and drops them to the forest floor, where the children quickly collect them. The party celebrates at the base of the tree by devouring some honeycomb, but ultimately the bulk of the treasure is divided among all of the pygmy families back at the village.

Similarly in Australia, Aborigines have, for thousands of years, hunted stingless honeybees (*Trigona* and *Austroplebia*, which they call "sugarbug") for their honey and propolis. Honey is, to this day, the backbone of Aborigines' diet and a mainstay in many of their rituals. Medicinally, they treat burns, lung ailments, eye infections, vomiting and diarrhea with honey.

Aboriginal honey hunters of northern Australia use their acute senses to locate trees that have hives within their trunks' hollow sections. Hunters search for a type of small, black lizard that lives near honey trees. These lizards pluck bees out of the air with their sticky tongues just before the bees enter the tree opening to their hive. Once the hive is located, the hunters chop notches into the trunk as footholds. Knocking on the bark with the back of their axes, they accurately determine, by the sound, the hive's location inside the tree cavity. They carve an opening to extract honeycomb and propolis. Once finished looting, the hunters repair the opening with mud so they can return in future months to the same hive.

Beeswax

Beeswax is a somewhat silent partner in the daily lives of people around the world. Each year, we use 20 million kilograms (44 million pounds) of beeswax – valued at $25-million. In fact, in 2007 Clorox paid almost a billion dollars for Burt's Bees, the specialty beeswax-based personal care products company. From cosmetics, stick colognes, antiperspirants, candies and dental impressions to the mouthpieces of didgeridoos, beeswax is often an important component. Your pool table has beeswax filling its screw holes and the seams between the slates. Beeswax thread is still preferred by shoemakers – and sailors – because of its durability and incredible resistance to weathering. Furniture and automobile polish, industrial lubricants, paint removers and even the frets on a two-stringed Philippine kutiyapi boat-lute – they all rely on the wax of the bees.

Made of fatty acids and hydrocarbons, beeswax melts at a low temperature of 66°C (151°F). The Roman Catholic Church uses about 1.4 million kilograms (3.1 million pounds) of beeswax in their candles each year, which are 49 per cent beeswax.

In Asia, many textiles are hand-painted using a technique called batik, or wax-resist. In the batik process, covering sections of a pattern with beeswax allows those sections to resist any dye that is later applied. The same batik method creates the intricate designs on pysanky – Ukrainian Easter eggs. Since the lightest-colour dye is applied first, beeswax (often mixed with some paraffin for a cracking effect on textiles) is applied to the areas intended to be that light colour. Once dry, the wax resists any subsequent darker-coloured dyes. At the end of the process, the designer melts the beeswax off to reveal the whole pattern. Indonesia, India, Malaysia and Thailand use the batik process, providing clothes for more than 1.5 billion people.

Unfortunately, beeswax is a sponge for toxic chemicals. Beehives exposed to CheckMite – a commercial pesticide used to kill *varroa*, a mite that is fatal to bees – results in beeswax contaminated with a carcinogenic organophosphate called coumaphos. Coumaphos is easily absorbed through the skin. Individuals exposed to this chemical experience a range of symptoms, including diminished lifespan, depending on the amount of exposure. This chemical infiltration into the bees' hive highlights the need to move beyond pesticides, herbicides, fungicides and miticides and toward a healthier future for both humans and bees.

Beyond the Hive & into the Future

As though the products of the beehive were not enough, humans are actively investigating even more ways to enrol bees to improve our well-being. Recent studies indicate that bees can count to four. With training, they appear to be able to count and return to a specific destination. While applications for their savvy number skills are yet untapped, many of their other distinct qualities – such as sight, smell and venom – are proving quite useful. For instance, research on bees' complete-picture eyesight has yielded results that may enable advances in miniaturized optics technology.

Bees' 170 smell receptors and nearly perfect accuracy hold potential as a diagnostic tool. Researchers, with the aim of enhancing early detection of disease, are currently training bees to detect pheromones and toxins specific to various cancers, diabetes and tuberculosis. By training bees to associate a specific smell with a desired resource, bees will, once trained, react to that distinctive odour by flying toward the source. For instance, odours in your breath – in a controlled environment so bees don't fly into your mouth – could provide primary indications of a yet undetectable disease.

With only a short olfactory training period, it is also possible to utilize bees' acute sense of smell to locate landmines (via the TNT residue), bombs and various chemicals. Bees currently work in conjunction with humans and dogs to pinpoint exact locations of such buried menaces. With between 80 and 120 million landmines – and counting – in over 70 countries, the value of this gift is immeasurable. Also, as these statically charged insects go about foraging, their bodies attract particles from the environment, essentially bringing a chemical and biological survey of the area back to their hive, granting us a glimpse into areas where it may be unsafe for humans to venture.

Since 1957, the former USSR has used extracts of bee stings – bee venom, known as apis – to treat rheumatoid arthritis, multiple sclerosis and other debilitating autoimmune diseases. Bee venom contains biochemicals that enhance blood flow to the damaged regions and block the perception of neuralgic pain. Currently dubbed apitherapy, apis treatment is on the rise throughout the world. Taking advantage of the anti-inflammatory effects of melittin and adolapin in bee venom – along with apamin to improve nerve transmission – apis can treat arthritis, fibromyalgia and tendonitis. In fact, 12 European countries have officially recognized bee venom solution as a drug.

Bees and Food Production

There are over 330 million mouths to feed in Canada and the United States alone. The honeybees are directly responsible for pollinating over $44-billion worth of food and commodities each year in both countries, including melons, gourds, pears, plums, peaches, kiwis, macadamias, sunflowers, canola, avocados, lettuce, broccoli and cotton. The beef and dairy industries rely on bees to pollinate the alfalfa and clover fields for feed. Even corporations such as Starbucks and General Mills – owner of Häagen-Dazs – rely on bees to pollinate their coffee and more than half of their ice cream ingredients.

Beekeepers are struggling to sustain themselves. With the wholesale price of honey hovering around US$3 per pound (2005–2009), they must rent out their colonies. About three million honeybee hives are used in food production in Canada and the US. In the US the scale and scope of the operation is mind boggling, given that many of the 2.4 million hives spend most of their time on trailers being trucked back and forth across the country.

Billions of bees travel great distances to pollinate entire harvests of almonds, apples, blueberries, cherries, cranberries, cucumbers, grapes and tomatoes, to name only a few more. For instance, a beekeeper may begin the season by having their bees pollinate citrus in Florida. They then may head north to do the blueberries and cranberries of Maine, then west to the Dakotas to pollinate clover and alfalfa. Perhaps a stop in Kansas or Missouri in the fall for goldenrod (which makes delicious honey) precedes their likely winter home in California to get ready for the enormous pollination effort on the almond plantations in early February.

Hives in Canada are not quite as nomadic. Alberta's beekeepers transport their hives into British Columbia to service the blueberry fields.

New Brunswick's blueberries use hives from Nova Scotia and Quebec for pollination.

The cotton industry in the US alone generates $27-billion in revenue through various sectors, including clothing, and food in the form of cottonseed oil, shortening, salad dressing, crackers, cookies and chips. Grown in 17 states on over 18,600 farms, cotton covers 4.2 million hectares (10.4 million acres) of land in the US. Despite the massive assistance bees provide for growing these crops, the cotton industry uses 34 million kilograms (75 million pounds) of pesticides each year. According to the US Environmental Protection Agency (EPA), a dozen of these pesticides are carcinogenic.

Almonds, for example

High in fibre, rich in vitamin E and loaded with antioxidants that help prevent heart disease and cancers, almonds are now one of the favourite nut varieties. Originally from Asia, both the almond and its close cousin the peach evolved to thrive in North America. While the peach offers a delicious, fleshy fruit with a stone-seed pit, the almond bears a thick, fibrous hull encasing the prized edible seed – the nut. California's Sacramento and San Joaquin valleys grow 82 per cent of the world's almonds – over 682 million kilograms (1.5 billion pounds).

Almond flowers require bees as their pollinator. To attain a bumper crop, 100 per cent of the flowers require pollination, which is unlikely to happen in the wild. Growers must graft at least a couple of varieties in their plantations because nature requires cross-pollination between varieties of almonds, not within a single variety. Almond growers are able to force this massive monoculture plantation (322,000 hectares or 796,000 acres) by densely loading onto their land about 550,000 honeybees per hectare (nearly a quarter million bees per acre). Over 1.5 million healthy hives – 75 billion bees – must apply their Herculean efforts to realize this astounding 100 per cent pollination mark.

In 2004, the almond growers were paying nearly $40 per hive. In 2006/07, after an enormous honeybee collapse, the price per hive

soared to $150. As bee populations continue to diminish, the escalating prices large-scale agriculture will have to pay for bees' services has vast economic implications. Not only does this development increasingly affect our smaller-scale farmers and the market prices we pay at retail, it also bolsters the drive to turn bees into even more of a commodity. Those who breed genetically modified bees or own the bulk of bee populations stand to profit greatly. For the rest of us, however, that potential signals a precarious future.

Industrial Agriculture: A Call for Change

Agriculture systems need to mimic the structure and function of indigenous ecosystems by working with the native plant communities. The grandfather of organic farming, Sir Albert Howard, understood that any agriculture system is only as good as its soil. Plant roots and soil are living, breathing, breeding communities of trillions of bacteria, fungi, protozoa, nematodes, micro-arthropods, worms, beetles and so much more. They decompose

recently died plant materials and add them to the humus layer, ensuring the structure, aeration and water retention of the soil. Plant roots also actively release food into the soil to promote micro-organism development.

Modern agriculture systems use chemical pesticides, fumigants, fungicides, herbicides and fertilizers that kill a vast range of beneficial micro-organisms. Micro-organisms promote healthy plant growth, boost plant defence mechanisms and naturally break down pollutants in the soil. In fact, conventional agriculture has reduced bacterial numbers from trillions per gram of soil in the root zone to a mere couple of million.

Weakened plants are obviously more susceptible to disease and infestations. In turn, the plants' weakness serves to justify further dependence on chemical pesticides. Of course, this continues to weaken and destroy the extremely diverse web of life in soil biology. To compound the problem, in North America alone over 500 agricultural pests are now resistant to our latest pesticides.

The Soil Foodweb Institute has identified and quantified these problems over years of research by a variety of specialists. The Institute has developed an excellent, economically viable solution to naturally nourish and rejuvenate soil ecosystems. After assessing soils for their deficiencies, the Institute brews up a compost tea – a liquid produced by leaching soluble nutrients and extracting bacteria, fungi, protozoa and nematodes from compost. The tea inoculates microbial life into the soil or onto the foliage of the crop plants, adding necessary soluble nutrients for foliar and soil ecosystems. The process invigorates both micro-organisms and plant life.

Globally, humans rely on about 20 plant species for our staple food source. Maintaining the soil food web of life is the *only* way our planet will be able to feed the burgeoning human population, by allowing for truly sustainable agriculture in the 21st century.

For over 20 years, the Land Institute in Kansas has examined the ecology of the Great Plains Grassland and broadened understanding

of nitrogen fixers, native plants, natural plant defence mechanisms and beneficial insects. Not surprisingly, these native communities work together to provide essential habitat for pollinators such as bumble and solitary bees, moths, bats and hummingbirds.

Nitrogen fixers are enriching members of the soil community. They are plants that take nitrogen gas from the air and, with the assistance of root bacterial nodules, add it into the soil. By using native nitrogen fixers in the field, there is no need for chemical-based nitrate fertilizers, which are inorganic salts that destroy the soil biology.

Native plants with both deep and shallow roots have adapted to different sources of moisture. Plant life on the Great Plains Grassland, including the renowned grasses, has figured out how to contend with aridity. The plants invest as much as 80 per cent of their growth into roots, promoting healthy soil biology. The Land Institute has documented over 230 native perennial plant species in Kansas that provide constant ground cover throughout the

growing season and soak up every drop from convectional downpours. Of the more than 230 documented plants, there are between 20 and 30 nitrogen fixers – nature's way of fertilizing the soil food web.

In Kansas, modern agriculture's monoculture fields of wheat experience eight times as much runoff as the wild prairie does. Considering this fact, the Land Institute has developed a system called polyculture. Polyculture mixes native species of plants in plots similar to how they exist in nature.

The Institute has found four particular crops that produce significantly greater yields compared to the local monoculture crops. The first is Eastern gama grass (*Tripsacum dactyloides*), a cousin of corn that makes terrific meal. Secondly, a legume eaten by livestock called Illinois bundle flower (*Desmanthus illinoensis*). Third is mammoth wild rye (*Leymus racemosus*), a close cousin of wheat that the Mongols successfully used during droughts. Finally, Maximilian's sunflower (*Helianthus maximiliana*) is an oil-rich seed able to supply vegetable oil or biodiesel. Not only are all four plants bio-logically compatible, but when planted together their combined yield skyrockets. Compatible species in nature provide each other with bio-chemical protection and moisture, a knockout one-two punch combination.

There are numerous other forward-thinking agriculture systems springing up around the globe. All of these movements have a significant role to play in guiding us away from the toxic future currently facing us and toward a path of self-sufficiency. Looking back and learning from our – often forgotten – natural environ-ments brings all life on our planet closer to a healthier existence.

Down a Path We Can't Sustain

Many ancient cultures revered bees for their honey, yet most had no idea of their overall global importance as partners in the plant kingdom. The Mayans are the notable exception. Almost 2,000 years ago, the Mayans very clearly understood that the health of the stingless bees was central to their very existence; they entrusted this protective role to their most sacred shaman.

One stingless beehive in Middle America requires about 482 square kilometres (186 square miles) of jungle to fill its comb with honey. The health of the jungle also depends on bees cross-pollinating. Stingless bees in particular evolved to pollinate the vanilla orchid, which yields a lucrative vanilla pod used as a spice. Deforestation and widespread use of insecticides have destroyed the bees' habitat, resulting in the extinction of the stingless honeybee populations in Mexico and Central America. Humans must now attempt to hand-pollinate these marvellous plants by peeling back a flap that is accessible for only one day a year.

Or consider springtime along the hillsides in the province of Sichuan, China. The pear trees transform an otherwise green landscape into a soft white, as a billion flowers grow. Well-documented carcinogens – organophosphate insecticides – are so prevalent that no beekeeper will venture into these plantations. The entire native bumble and solitary bee populations are dead from years of toxicity. In turn, thousands of migrant workers – including women and children – dangle from the pear tree limbs as they attempt to hand-pollinate each flower.

Yet, we do not have to look back in time or outside of our own backyard to discuss the devastation of ecosystems – including our beloved bees. In Europe, Canada and the United States, honeybee populations have plummeted dramatically over the past few years. In late 2006, beekeepers discovered – almost overnight – millions of nearly abandoned hives with no trace of any dead bodies. Colony Collapse Disorder (CCD) is the name of this widespread and ongoing condition. Hives suffering from CCD are loaded with brood (immature bees) and honeycomb, but only the queen and a few workers remain; all are very nervous and completely disoriented.

Bee populations are suffering throughout the world. In the UK over the past century, the number of beehives has reportedly declined by nearly 75 per cent, from over a million to 280,000. Between September 2008 and early April 2009, honeybee colonies in the US declined by 29 per cent according to a study by the US Department of Agriculture. Despite increased awareness and research, 29 per cent is only a slight improvement from the previous two years. The decline in Canadian honeybee numbers over the past three years is similar to that in the US.

While the media desperately sought a smoking gun, they lost sight of the marvellous complexity of biological systems. Scientists endeavour to discover and understand pieces of the rich tapestry of life. Yet, when applied science attempts to solve problems in ecosystems, it is very difficult to find a single cause and effect. It is always more likely that a number of factors – acting together – cause a breakdown. Thus, the answer to why billions of bees are disappearing worldwide is not one single "smoking gun," but a whole arsenal.

Research into the causes of CCD is focusing on the following areas: pathogens and parasites, bee management stresses like poor nutrition, and environmental stresses such as pesticides. While there is no causal relationship established yet, we will briefly consider some of the armaments in the above research categories that may be working in concert to debilitate the bee populations.

The honeybees have one distinct advantage that emboldens hope for their plight. In 2006, their genome was fully decoded. Knowing the nearly ten thousand genes of the honeybee opens up vast potential for research into

CCD and its related causes. For instance, the decoded genome reveals that honeybees have only half as many genes for detoxification and immunity as other insects. Interestingly, bees from around the globe have the same sets of "good" bacteria inside their stomachs and intestines. These specific bacteria are unique to bees and are of paramount importance for bees to fight pathogens and detoxify pesticides.

A University of Illinois research team recently (2009) compared the genome of healthy hives and hives suffering from CCD in two geographical regions. Particularly, they looked at the genes active in the stomachs and intestines and consistently found atypical fragments of ribosomal RNA in CCD-afflicted bees. Such damage to ribosomes impacts protein production and the health of the bee as a whole. With compromised ribosomes, the bee cannot produce the necessary proteins to effectively act against parasites, viruses, pesticides and other threats. Honeybees are currently suffering extremely high disease loads such as deformed wing virus, Israeli acute paralysis virus, sac-brood virus, black queen cell virus, Kashmir bee virus and others – 14, to be exact. In general, higher viral loads are consistently present in colonies suffering from CCD. Whether this phenomenon is a potential cause or a potential effect of an already weakened immune system is a current topic of investigation.

A lot of attention has been given to the Israeli acute paralysis virus (IAPV), which causes bees to shiver until paralysis and death. Since 2002 in the US, the virus has mutated at least twice from its original Israeli form. Both Canada and the US import hundreds of thousands of honeybees from Australia. The Israeli virus was found on some Australian honeybees in 2006/07 and was – again – incorrectly diagnosed as the single cause of CCD. Current research suggests that IAPV is still considered one of the factors involved in CCD.

Varroa destructor is a voracious microscopic mite that originated in Asia. After attacking the Asian honeybee (*Apis cerana*), the mites jumped cargo ships and hitchhiked into Florida, arriving in 1987. Since then, they have wreaked havoc throughout North America (and elsewhere), killing millions of honeybee colonies. Tracheal and *varroa* mites cause immuno-suppression in bees by secreting a substance that prevents the bees from producing the enzymes and antimicrobial peptides that usually fend off invasion. Recent research suggests that this carrier of picorna-like viruses may initiate ribosome breakdown. Attempts to provide protection with a number of fluvalinate pesticides, including Apistan and CheckMite – recall that this chemical also contaminates beeswax – have only resulted in the mites developing resistance. So far, only Hawaii and Australia are free of these destructive mites.

Another parasite attacking bees is *Nosema ceranae* – a parasitic fungus that first afflicted the Asian honeybee. Discovered in the early 1990s in North America and in 2003 in Europe, the fungus was also once falsely accused as the sole cause of CCD. *Nosema* infiltrates a bee's intestines, where the fungus nuclei divide repeatedly and produce organisms. This process destroys the bee's digestive system. The antibiotic fumagillin is the regular treatment for hives infected with this fungus, a treatment that is also linked to the dramatic increase in disease loads, as it weakens the bees' immune systems.

In North America and elsewhere, our captive honeybees are being overworked and undernourished. In the US, honeybees are exposed to toxic endocrine-disrupting chemicals and fed high-fructose corn syrup and monoculture pollen. Beekeepers around the globe are attempting to combat this management stress on bees by changing the food they provide for their hives. One example of this is a form of protein shake that consists of eggs, brewer's yeast, pollen, honey and other special ingredients.

Poor nutrition is also impacting non-captive bees through a combination of environmental stresses. For instance, the abnormally high temperatures of 2006 were quite likely the tipping point for the bees in North America. The searingly hot springtime, right during the onset of flowering, may have caused sterile pollen in many plants. In 2007, tests of almond, plum, kiwi and cherry pollen revealed little, if any, protein content. Infertile soils lacking essential nutrients, bacteria, fungi and protozoa – along with climate change – worked together to cause this phenomenon.

Before we wade into the environmental stress caused by pesticides, it is worth mentioning the debilitating effect of electromagnetic radiation on bees. Cellular phone towers emit high frequencies of radiation as they provide coverage across landmasses. Research from Europe determined that bees exposed to this form of radiation made 21 per cent less honeycomb. Furthermore, only 36 per cent of radiation-exposed bees taken 800 metres (½ mile) from their hive were able to navigate home. This research made great waves in the press, but recently the head researcher of the project issued a statement that there is no established causal link between his findings on electromagnetic radiation and CCD.

Pesticides and the damage done

Each year, our global biosphere endures an onslaught of some 2.3 billion kilograms (5 billion pounds) of pesticides. Many of these pesticides are neonicotinoids, which synthetically mimic a plant compound found in tomatoes, potatoes, peppers and tobacco. A neuro-active insecticide fashioned after nicotine, neonicotinoids poison nerves and prevent acetylcholine from enabling neurons to communicate with each other and with muscle tissue. In humans, for instance, these substances would trigger Parkinson's and Alzheimer's diseases.

A subsidiary of the pharmaceutical company Bayer (the Aspirin people), called Bayer CropScience, manufactures the pesticides clothianidin (called Poncho in Europe) and imidacloprid (called Gaucho in France). They are forms of neonicotinoid. In France in 1999, a third of the honeybee population died due to the use of Gaucho. Over the next five years, authorities progressively banned its use on selected crops, and in 2008 Gaucho was banned altogether. In 2008, Germany too banned eight neonicotinoid seed-treatment products, including Poncho, because of the devastating impact they have on bee populations.

Bayer representatives claim that application errors were to blame for the chemicals ending up in the air and affecting bees. That said, warning labels on these pesticides indicate the following – familiar – post-exposure symptoms: memory loss, appetite loss, disorientation and immune system collapse. Despite all the controversy and evidence, these products are still widely used throughout North America.

In Canada, beekeepers in New Brunswick and Prince Edward Island have experienced serious declines in their bee populations – between 50 and 80 per cent colony loss since 1999. These beekeepers believe that imidacloprid – under the trade name Admire – is responsible. The chemical residues collect in the pollen and nectar of crops that are pollinated by honeybees. In turn, bees repeatedly ingest the chemicals and slowly die. Similar concerns have been raised in Ontario potato farming areas.

In 2008, researchers from Penn State University found evidence of 43 different pesticide varieties in Pennsylvania apple orchards. Some farmers "stack" chemicals – that is, mix them together in a single broadcast application. The US EPA has no data on stacking. They rely on Bayer, BASF, Dow, Monsanto, DuPont and Syngenta to do all the safety tests. The EPA does not conduct independent tests of herbicides, pesticides, fungicides and miticides unless a worthy calamity occurs.

Even more disturbing are results from mixing a neonicotinoid with the fungicide Procure. Procure combats powdery mildew on melons, squash, pumpkins, cucumbers, zucchini, apples, pears, strawberries and cherries – all pollinated plants. Mixing increases toxicity to honeybees more than a thousandfold. The gross overuse of herbicides, pesticides, fungicides and miticides – individually and stacked – drastically weakens bees' autoimmune systems.

The present agriculture system uses so much pesticide that if the stuff were packed in 45-kilogram (99-pound) sacks, it would encircle the entire planet. Clearly, industrial-scale agriculture desperately needs restructuring. When that deleterious system combines with climate change and a beleaguered worldwide bee population, we know this is not the best way forward. Today more than ever, we need to respect nature and interpret her warning signposts – such as billions of dying bees. Change is opportunity in disguise. By aiming to work within nature's blueprint, our species has a golden opportunity to flourish in the 21st century.

How To Help the Bees Recover

Businesses involved with agriculture – directly or indirectly – are responsible for forcing the most stress on our ecosystems, but they also have the resources to improve the situation. While we actively wait for them to realize the benefits of answering calls for change, it is at the local level that each of us has the power to act. In various segments of society, there are movements to protect our environment. There are many ways to take action and participate in making our world a healthier place – for bees, humans and life as a whole.

Conservation biology, for instance, is a relatively new branch in science; its mandate is to protect the genetic tapestry of life on Earth. Life on land and under the sea holds the cure for every disease. In fact, an entire new industry with legions of engineers and scientists has cropped up, called biomimicry. Biomimicry uses nature's own innovations to solve engineering, materials science and medical problems. While not all of us are scientists, this does not stop us from tapping into the incredibly important research that is happening all around us. From a quick Google search for information to getting involved with projects in your area, you too can participate by increasing your understanding of the issues.

Recently, us First Lady Michelle Obama created an organic garden on the White House lawn. Right next to it are two honeybee hives with an official "keeper." New surges of urban beekeepers are making headlines around the world. Yet, we do not have to keep bees in order to nurture and protect them. There are actions to take in multiple areas of our lives that will help to respect – and give back to – the incomparable honeybees that give so much to us. After all, we are inextricably linked in this dance of planetary survival.

It is not unimaginable that the honeybees could be yet another vital resource that gets commodified eventually. Imagine having to order and pay to have bees brought to your garden to pollinate. Or what would the price of food be once only a handful of corporations hold the "patent" or "licence" for all remaining (or genetically modified) honeybees? While these ideas may seem extreme, we need only look to the decade-long litigation between agribusiness giant Monsanto and local Saskatchewan farmers Percy and Louise Schmeiser. This farm couple's legal battle illustrates how the corporations responsible for vigorously promoting modified crops and the use of chemicals could end up ultimately profiting from the eventual total decline of the species they quietly help to destroy.

In the end, consider all that you have learned about the bees – their history and current status. While they continually give to us, humans have regrettably neglected our dynamic little friends. Here is a list of ways you can help the bees. Let's hope that next year's reports show bee populations increasing from their currently depleted numbers.

Things a person can do:

- ○ Buy organic foods.
- ○ Buy organic cotton.
- ○ Support your local beekeepers by purchasing organic honey.
- ○ Do not use herbicides, pesticides, fungicides or miticides in your yard. When insecticides are necessary, the Indian neem tree is a wonderful natural powerhouse. Neem-based products do not harm bees, moths, bats, hummingbirds or any other beneficial insect such as spiders, ladybugs, dragonflies. Neem products don't harm any warm-blooded animals or birds either.
- ○ Plant a wide variety of native flowers – especially yellows and blues in solid blocks of 1 × 1 metres (3 × 3 feet) so that bees can see them.
- ○ Provide somewhere for bees to live in your yard, such as dead tree branches, old animal burrows or wooden bee blocks.

- Visit the website of the USDA Agriculture Research Service Logan Bee Lab for details on bee-friendly wild flowers: www.ars.usda.gov/Services/docs.htm?docid=12052.
- To find out how to build a pollinator garden, visit www.pollinator.org.
- Let some of your garden's leafy plants go to seed at the end of the season; they'll provide food for some species of bees before the colder months.
- Bees need water, too, so place a bowl with water in your yard and replenish it regularly.
- If in Illinois, join Bee Spotter and help scientists learn what species are in your area: http://beespotter.mste.uiuc.edu . If not in Illinois, check out the Bee Spotter site and consider starting one for your own area.

Climate change has dramatically affected plants by speeding up the timing of flowering. Native bees and other pollinators time their awakening in the spring with floral blooms. If pollinators incorrectly time their spring emergence and miss the bloom, both plants and animals perish. Thousands of volunteers are helping plant scientists and beekeepers track the timing of local blooms.

- In Canada, consider participating in one of the "watch" programs through Nature Watch: www.icewatch.ca/english.
- For specific provinces, find the plant watch organizations that you can "get involved" with – such as in Alberta, at http://plant watch.fanweb.ca/.
- If in the US, consider participating in the National Phenology Network: www.usanpn.org.
- Support organizations that protect wildland habitat, e.g., Nature Conservancy, Ducks Unlimited, Conservation International, The Land Conservancy or other, local agencies.
- Visit the From the Soil Up website and get tips on working with natural systems: www.fromthesoilup.com.au.

- Support the increase in grazing cows by purchasing free-range beef. Grazing cows do not require (much if any) Tylosin or other antibiotics, and vacant fields are crucial habitat for bumble and solitary bees.
- Consider supporting organizations such as Bees Without Borders www.beeswithout borders.org/.

There is a worldwide movement afoot to follow nature's blueprint. Get curious and get involved!

Further Reading

Benjamin, Allison, and Brian McCallum. *A World without Bees*. London: Pegasus Books, 2009.

Bishop, Holley. *Robbing the Bees: A Biography of Honey, The Sweet Liquid Gold that Seduced the World*. New York: Free Press, 2005.

Buchmann, Stephen, and Banning Repplier. *Letters from the Hive: An Intimate History of Bees, Honey, and Humankind*. New York: Bantam, 2005.

Crane, Eva, and Harold Pager. *The Rock Art of Honey Hunters*. Cardiff: International Bee Research Association, 2001.

Halter, Reese. *Wild Weather*. Canmore, Alta.: Altitude Publishers, 2007.

Maeterlinck, Maurice. *The Life of the Bee*. New York: New American Library, Mentor Books, 1954. First published 1901 by Blue Ribbon Books.

Savage, Candace Sherk. *Prairie: A Natural History*. Vancouver: David Suzuki Foundation: Greystone Books/Douglas & McIntyre, 2004. [Berkeley, Calif.]: Distributed in US by Publishers Group West.

Schoenherr, Allan A. *A Natural History of California.*
Berkeley: University of California Press, 1992.

Seeley, Thomas D. *The Wisdom of the Hive: The Social
Physiology of Honey Bee Colonies.* Cambridge, Mass.:
Harvard University Press, 1995.

von Frisch, Karl. *The Dancing Bees: An Account of the Life and
Senses of the Honey Bee.* 1st US ed. New York: Harcourt,
Brace, 1955. Originally published as *Aus dem Leben der
Bienen.* Berlin, Göttingen, Heidelberg: Springer Verlag,
1953.

Wilson, Edward O. *Sociobiology: The New Synthesis.*
Cambridge, Mass.: Belknap Press of Harvard University
Press, 1975.

About the Author

Dr. Reese Halter is an award-winning conservation biologist, syndicated science writer, TV host and father. He is a sought-after public speaker and founder of the international conservation institute Global Forest Science, through which he regularly visits schools and encourages children worldwide to embrace conservation, science exploration and learning. Dr. Reese lives in Los Angeles, California, and can be contacted through www.DrReese.com.

Other Titles in this Series

The Weekender Effect

Hyperdevelopment in Mountain Towns

Robert William Sandford

As cities continue to grow at unprecedented rates, more and more people are looking for peaceful, weekend retreats in mountain or rural communities. More often than not, these retreats are found in and around resorts or places of natural beauty. As a result, what once were small towns are fast becoming mini-cities, complete with expensive housing, fast food, traffic snarls and environmental damage, all with little or no thought for the importance of local history, local people and local culture. *The Weekender Effect* is a passionate plea for considered development in these communities and for the necessary preservation of local values, cultures and landscapes.

ISBN-13: 978-1897522103

Denying the Source

The Crisis of First Nations Water Rights

Merrell-Ann S. Phare

The demands for access to waters that First Nations depend upon are intense and growing. Oil and gas, mining, ranching, farming and hydro development all require enormous quantities of water, and each brings its own set of negative impacts to the rivers, lakes and groundwater sources that are critical to First Nations. Climate change threatens to make matters even worse. This book is a call to respect the water rights of First Nations, and in doing so, to create a new water ethic in Canada and beyond.

ISBN-13: 978-1897522615

RMB saved the following resources by printing
the pages of this book on chlorine-free paper
made with 100% post-consumer waste:

Trees · 7, fully grown

Water · 3,021 gallons

Solid Waste · 183 pounds

Greenhouse Gases · 627 pounds

Calculations based on research by Environmental Defense and
the Paper Task Force. Manufactured at Friesens Corporation.